Volume 1: printing with updates

Chayil Ishah – Exposing the Lie

Ending Domestic Abuse Through the Power of Truth

Written By
Cheryl A Gidding MH, Th.D

Charcoal Drawings
By Maryne Bethea

Copyright © 2010 Cheryl A. Gidding

Cover Picture by Maryne Bethea
Cover Design by Cheryl Gidding
Drawings by Maryne

All rights reserved.
No part of this book may be reproduced in any form without permission in writing from the author.

PO Box 731, San Juan Bautista, Ca. 95045-0731

First Printing: 1/2011
Second Printing 3/2013

ISBN-13: 978-1456497965

United States

Dedication:

The book is first dedicated to YHWH for His abundant, eternal love and truth because the truth really can set one free and heal broken hearts, lives and spirits.

This book is secondly dedicated to, and written for, all the women of the world who have suffered and endured the many kinds of abuses and cruelties of the world in both religious and secular societies, and individual homes.

It is with genuine sorrow I think of those who have suffered and/or died in the past through abuse, and those who are enduring now – yet it is with love, hope and encouragement that I offer this book to all women of every age, race, and background that you may be truly free through truth rather than remaining in the bondage of the religious traditions of mankind.

Thank You To:

I first thank my husband, Mike, for his love, loyalty and support. With all love to you, Mike – you are the best of the best – I love you very much - thank you!

I also thank Maryne for her amazing support and understanding; and mutually shared passion for sharing the truth and love of YHWH to all women helping to break the bondage of abuse. I also thank you so very much for your amazing drawings for this series as a picture can indeed say a thousand words – they are simply beautiful - and for your friendship!

You are an amazing, intelligent, talented, courageous and insightful woman and friend, hugs and love to you always!

I send out a special thank you to my mother and father, Jackie and Bob (*Who went on to YHWH on 12-3-2007)* for all the encouragement and opportunity you gave me, for encouraging education in many areas of life, for teaching me compassion for others, and to love all His creations from early on. I love you, Mom!

And to Rass - because you have blessed my mother's heart in so many ways!

There are many others also who have touched my life, helped me to grow and mature, been my friend; laughed and cried, rejoiced with me and encouraged me to keep seeking, keep climbing and to never give up – to my sisters and to my friends, thank you and hugs!

And a special thank you to Betsy for her honest editing and critiquing of this work. 'Very' appreciated. Love you!

May YHWH bless all who read the words of this book, and may He bless all who hear the Word in these that I share.

Cheryl Gidding

Contents

Introduction……..9

Chapter1 - The Truth about Abuse - 13

Chapter 2 - The Key of Knowledge - 21

Chapter 3 - You are not Alone – Statistics - 30

Chapter 4 – A Common Root - 39

Chapter 5 – The Creation of Woman - 48

Chapter 6 – Exposing the Lie - 58

Chapter 7 – A Touch Like Silk - 73

Chapter 8 – Healing the Broken Hearted - 91

Psalms116 - 104

It is time – 106

Notes - 109

Revision Notes:

The revisions/updates made in this book do not change its content, meaning nor purpose. The following are the basic updates you will see in this printing, mostly having to do with the scripture translation being used.

1. I have replaced the previous scripture translation with a more commonly known one. There were many factors leading to this decision however, the two main reasons are integrity of resources used, and familiarity.

2. In addition it is my firm belief that one can learn to dig for truth in any translation if one has the right tools and tips to do it.

3. I have chosen to use the KJV for the scriptures. Not due to its accuracy however, as it has many translation errors in it. Rather, the reasoning was twofold. **A**: *It is one of the most commonly known; and most folks have either the KJV or a similar translation in their possession.* **B:** *Through showing what is traditionally taught based on the KJV, versus the ancient and more correct translations of key words regarding women in scripture, one can more easily learn how to dig for these*

truths on their own rather than having to blindly follow tradition. **YHWH's Word has not changed, Mankind has changed His written Word.**

4. In all scripture, I have replaced the term 'The LORD' with His proper name as is found in the oldest text known and proven, and, as close to accuracy in transliteration into English as possible. Therefore you will see **'YHWH'** in its place and the difference is explained.

5. I have placed in parenthesis the proper translation of a few key words within the scriptures themselves for more accurate understanding of the point being made.

Beyond this, there have been no changes made to the content of this book other than a couple of spelling/grammar errors; and, a comment or two that was needed due to the using the KJV.

Introduction:

Men <u>and</u> women are born to be free thinking, free living, free choosing human beings. The freedom we are given is for a special purpose, it is not for selfish gain, nor for cruel domination, but rather because true love, genuine love, is given and received freely from the heart both to our Creator and, to each other.

True love, whether to another human being or to our Creator cannot be forced, coerced, bought, manipulated or brainwashed into existence or brought about by fear.

<u>True</u> love comes only from a free heart and mind, and true love does no intentional harm! Women, as well as men, were born to be free.

Scripture tells us that the whole world has been deceived. In many ways, it has, and the subject of women is one of them. My hope and prayer is that by revealing the correct translation of words/definitions, and the genuine love that the Creator has for His daughters as opposed to the traditional teachings about women, you will be set firmly on the path to freedom from abuse, violence and oppression, in more ways than one; more ways than you had hoped, just as I was, and beyond.

In this first book of the Chayil Ishah series, we will look at two of the most commonly mistranslated and misunderstood passages in scripture regarding women in addition to statistics and encouragements.

We are also going to look at some of the most devastating effects of these mistranslations and false teachings along with some of the foundational truths surrounding them.

I am one who knows that trimming the tip of a massive poison oak bush will not stop the spread of it, and painting it to look like a rose won't last. Rather, it must be dug out at the root with new, strong life planted in its place. This is the approach of this first book in a very needed series for not just women, but men also.

Placing restrictions on women through faulty traditional religious teachings, also restricts the blessings of those around them including husbands and families as whole.

Billions of children over the centuries who grow up in households where women are belittled, controlled, abused and dominated forcefully, tend to either grow into adulthood as abusers, or being abused themselves. In other cases they oft times simply grow into adulthood having a very warped sense of what love really is and/or how to give and receive it joyfully and with beauty.

The world has also missed out on the potentially brilliant contributions of women because of these false beliefs, many of which are based on faulty interpretations of scripture due to inaccurate and biased translations through the centuries.

Before continuing I must say that this writing and all future writings by me are not intended to blame or point fingers, cause destructive uprisings, demonize or cause hatred towards men, religions or societies in any way, shape or form – rather they are intended to simply speak the truth in love.

As you go through this series it is my hope and prayer that women will begin to see that not only have both men <u>and</u> women in religious settings perpetuated this problem, but also that rather than spending time trying to point fingers at people, women will begin to simply start making choices in life according to the truth and love of the Word rather than incorrect translation which will allow you the freedom to be who YHWH created you to be, in love, wisdom, courage and strength.

May you be blessed and encouraged; and, may you find hope and freedom in the awesome truth of YHWH's love for you – a truth that <u>rarely</u> gets told.

Cheryl Gidding MH, Th.D

Chapter 1

The Truth About Abuse

Many teachings regarding women, both religious and secular, give the idea that women are less important, less capable and less intelligent; that we are designed to obey only and not to think and do also. Incorrectly translated scripture/writings, have perpetuated these false ideas. Here and now I am choosing to openly and boldly speak the truth in this matter and pray with all sincerity that many will be set free.

Whether subtle or direct, these ideas have permeated religions and societies all over the world. In my own seeking for truth, peace, love, and freedom, I discovered that the scriptures that have been handed down to us for centuries have been altered - yes, altered. The first revelation of this came by hearing His actual Name for the first time instead of hearing the ever popular phrase, 'The LORD'.

Even when not altered, it has oft times been misunderstood due to Western angles of thinking vs. ancient Eastern thought, and also by the bias and influence of those who have used the scriptures for political power and/or simply power control reasons.

But tradition does not always equal truth and

when it comes to the subject of women facing abuse because of nothing more than man-made traditions it can, and often is, a matter of life and death for hundreds of millions of women.

When I began seeking truth and studying His Word with all my heart, mind, YHWH given intelligence, sincere seeking and strength regarding the Word to, and about, women (*and more*), what I found was a far cry from anything I had ever heard before! I suddenly found the door to healing, freedom and genuine love had been opened and hope returned after having been long stolen through various abuses in life .

2 Tim. 1:7 For God *(YHWH)* **has not given us a spirit of fear; but of power, and of love, and of a sound mind** *(self-control, balance of mind)*

My hope and prayer is that through learning the truth of His Word, women will learn what it is to live in the power, love and sound mind that the Father gives us; to be able to find and experience the peace that truly does surpass understanding.

As a very small but important example, did you know that the word 'oikorous' (*translated as 'housekeeper' in Titus 2:5)* has nothing to do with cleaning a house? It means to guard and protect the home, family and all who enter therein in a powerful way, both spiritually and physically. And yet, the average church teaches that it *does* mean to clean the home.

It is a very deceptive mistranslation. The word 'housekeeper' should be used in the same context as 'gatekeeper'. Would we assume that the word 'gatekeeper' means to 'clean gates'? Of course not. We realize it means to be a guard at a gate. Why then do we not realize the same with the word 'housekeeper'? Simply put, the answer to this question is that, regarding scripture, a false teaching by religious authorities and translators and power seeking people has become tradition and is swallowed blindly by many without any thought as to whether or not it is correct or true.

Now don't get me wrong here, there is nothing wrong with cleaning our homes of course. I clean my home and hope that you clean yours also; however, to teach women that the entire purpose of their life is to wash dishes is grossly incorrect, and as I mentioned earlier, the world has lost out on the blessings of the potentially brilliant contributions of women for centuries because of attempting to keep women confined to the duties of cleaning the home and cleaning up after their families.

I simply must add one extra word here – many people see those who clean the home as having 'easy' work – well let me tell you, it is not. The bending, lifting, scrubbing dirty work of keeping a home clean is not easy work at all and it takes genuine know-how to do it well as with any profession. However, to teach, or try to convince women, that the only thing they should desire to do in life is this kind of work - is just as absurd as expecting all men to enjoy and desire nothing more than to wash dishes or clean house.

We are unique individuals with unique talents and each has been given something special to pursue and develop. YHWH has given every person on the face of the planet, including women, the heart's desire to learn, grow, discover…and create as we <u>all</u> have been made in His image and likeness.

Being able to explore and develop something that is unique to our individuality is a blessing and gift of joy from YHWH. To prevent a woman from doing what YHWH created and gifted her to do, isto step between YHWH and His daughter and literally take His gift to her, away from her. And that, is just wrong. Who of any of us would appreciate being given a special gift and having someone take it from us?

And I must wonder if men really realize what they are doing in this? They are basically saying that they are more capable and more knowledgeable about women than YHWH is. Whoa! That is one frightening statement. I for one would never want to tell anyone that I know better than YHWH or that it is my right to take His gift to you away from you. Wow.

One result of this mess that people have made of the scriptures, which are beautiful in their <u>original meaning</u>, is that many women have turned away from faith in any kind of Creator because most (*not all*) churches teach the same message to women regarding total submission even in abusive, oppressive or otherwise harmful situations.

Hypocrisy, greed and abuse has abounded in religions for as long as 'religions' have been practiced. It is time to turn back the tide and get back to the beauty and love of the original Word of the Creator according to correctly translated scripture.

It is not only devastating to women but truly breaks my heart that the Words of our loving, Creator YHWH and His message of honor and genuine love have been warped so much so, that loving, intelligent people reject and turn on Him when it was really mankind who twisted and changed His written Word.

YHWH's Word has not changed, Mankind changed the written Word.

Millions of other women have learned to suppress themselves because they have been trained *(brainwashed)* to believe that it is the will of the Almighty to do so, and so they sadly live out their lives without ever knowing what it means to really grow, learn and feel the joy of being who YHWH created them to be, individually, uniquely, beautifully, in freedom.

John *(YHWchanon)* **4:23-24 But the hour comes, and now is, when true worshippers shall worship the Father in spirit and in truth: for the Father seeks such to worship him. God** *(YHWH)* **is Spirit: and those who worship him must worship him in spirit and, in truth.**

Abuse and/or betrayal in any form is not okay with YHWH according to His Word. The perpetuation of abuse towards women because of the false teachings and faulty interpretations of scripture must stop. Both men and women are beautiful creations of YHWH designed to live together, love each other, honor each other and love YHWH as one; with no abuse, no hatred, no harm and no unfaithfulness in any way, shape or form.

True love and wisdom seeks peace in all things – not destruction, power over others or causing anyone to feel 'less-than' just to make self feel more powerful or important.

Romans 13:10 **Love works no ill** *(harm, to make someone feel worthless, evil, destruction)* **to his neighbor: therefore love is the fulfilling of the law.**

For a married couple, the closest neighbor we have is our spouse. Genuine love does no intentional harm – period. Therefore any husband who attempts to control, manipulate, threaten, beat or coerce their wives into total submission – which 'does' cause deep and lingering harm – is doing the exact opposite of what genuine love it according to the Word.

Galatians 3:26-29 *For you are all the children of God* (YHWH) *by faith in* *(The anointed – Messiah - YHWshua)* *For as many of you as have been baptized into* *(the anointed – Messiah)* *have put on* *(the anointed – Messiah)* *There is neither Jew* (YHWDH) *nor Greek, there is neither bond nor free, there is neither male nor female: for you are all one in* *(the anointed Messiah YHWshua). And if you be* *(the Messiah's), then are you Abraham's seed, and heirs according to the promise.*

John 8:32 *And you will know the truth, and the truth will make you free* (It is important to take note that the verse previous to this, says if *we continue in 'His' Word. It is also of upmost importance to realize that 'His' Word is one of genuine love, His genuine original Word to humans was not politicized, warped nor used to control others – mankind did that)*

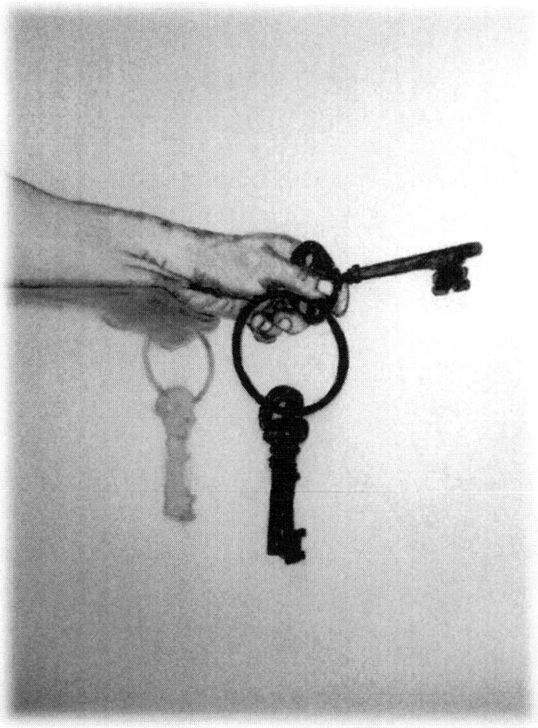

Chapter 2

The Key of Knowledge and Truth

<u>Luke 11:52</u> - **Woe to you, lawyers** *(Experts in religious law),* **for you have taken away the key of knowledge: you entered not in yourselves, and them that were entering in - you hindered.** *(prevented, blocked)*

The first thing that needs to be corrected and shared/explained is the *Key of Knowledge* according to Scripture. Just what is the Key of Knowledge according to Scripture? <u>It is His Name</u>. This may seem unimportant to some of you when it is the truth and healing of abuse that you may be seeking.

However, I share it for two reasons. Firstly, there are many misguided ideas of about His Name in relation to denominations, cults, groups, religions languages and more. Often people associate one particular English spelling to one group while another to another group with some of these groups having some downright cultish airs about them.

These ideas can often repel folks from seeking any further due to intended fear tactics in the wrong direction. Well, I have been through the fires of His Name in relationship to groups and denominations and would like to share with you when it's simple, direct from scripture and straight forward – it frees rather than creates fear because it points to no group, religion or denomination, but only to YHWH Himself; and, it makes simple clear sense.

Secondly, once one realizes that even His very Name Has been changed by the translators of old who sought political power – then the many other changes that have been made in these scriptures begins to come to life and are much easier seen and understood.

So let's look at His Name. In most, not all, translations you will see the words 'The LORD' *(in capital letters)* when referring to the Creator. Most believe that this is simply the meaning of the 'Hebrew' word YHWH. But this is not so.

The ancient *(and modern)* word for 'lord' is 'adonai' and it is spelled ADNY (ינדא), not YHWH (הוהי). They are two completely different words. The first one is a common word for 'lord or master' and the second, is the Name above all Names, the Name of the Creator YHWH. In fact many modern day bibles will have a small comment the front or back that explains this fact. But few read it.

There are many groups, pastors, educators and more, each with a different English rendering of His Name in English and, each 100% sure their particular rendering is the correct one. It can make it rather confusing for most.

It is not my intention to convince you of any one particular English spelling or pronunciation, nor to try and direct anyone to one particular group, denomination or religion; but rather, to YHWH and His love for you.

Therefore, in order to focus on what this book is about, His healing love and truth for women who have been abused, it is my decision to render His Name in English, just as it is found in the ancient scriptures: YHWH

Others believe, also because of incorrect translation and teachings, that it is just one of His 'many' Names - It is not. Time and time again, scripture tells us clearly, He has only one Name and it is YHWH.

Zackariah (ZakarYHW) **14:9** *And YHWH shall be king over all the earth: in that day shall there be one YHWH, and his name one* (echad: united).

His Name was removed from scripture literally thousands of times. Initially it was due to the fact that some priests seriously did not want to take His Name in vain *(to consider it as having little or no value)* or to be used too much and therefore make it nothing but a common word that most would not even understand.

However, over time, several additional things also occurred which further placed YHWH's

Name in hard to reach or know, places for the average population. In addition to His Name, the names of prophets, names of others, names of festivals and set apart times, the dates for those events and more have been altered in the English translations.

As time passed, His name, YHWH became more and more unknown as the Name 'YHWH' was purposefully removed from scripture with the intention of controlling populations *(political/power reasons)*.

This however does not mean that all who use these altered translations are willfully using something that had been changed, but rather most have simply been deceived and misled just as I was for many decades.

Those who know the truth but continue to teach a falsehood, well, I suppose only YHWH knows why they would do such a thing; however, false is false and to knowingly and willingly teach a lie is to not care about those whom they are teaching; in addition to breaking a foundational Word that offers 'trust' – the 9th commandment.

I once confronted a Pastor from the Gulf Coast in Texas whom I had heard teach a falsehood to the congregation only to hear the first of many stunning 'excuses' for it. I met with him, showed him what scripture actually said about the subject and then waited for his response.

He leaned back in his chair, arms behind his head, chuckled and said, *"What difference does it make? People don't care, I just keep them happy."*

And there-in my friends lies a huge problem. Much is taught that is not true, much goes unnoticed because people don't really care and/or they assume if a pastor says it, it 'must' be true; and so the traditions and lies get passed on down the line unopposed, unquestioned and unaddressed. This book, along with everything else I do – strongly opposes being lied to and strongly opposes the false teachings.

The Name of the Son has also been changed. Most people know the Name as 'Jesus' and believe it means 'to save'. Some of you may have been taught that the Name 'Jesus' is an English rendering of the Name 'Joshua', this is not exactly correct either, but close.

The Name given to Him when He was born was YHWshua. The Name Joshua correctly spelled in scripture is YHWshua.

What does YHWshua mean? It is really two words put together. The first portion of His Name is YHW *(Yah-oo)* which is a portion of the Name YHWH, our Creator. The second half of His Name is shua and it means to save, to rescue. It comes from a much deeper meaning that says *'When a predator is after the sheep, they will call out. Then, the shepherd will hear the cries of the sheep and rescue them'*. When you put it all together the Name of the Savior is YHWshua and it means <u>YHW saves/rescues</u>. He is the good shepherd.

Joel *(YHW El)* **2:32 And it shall come to pass, that whosoever shall call on the name of YHWH , shall be delivered:……**

Acts 2:21 And it shall come to pass, that whosoever shall call on the name of YHWH , shall be saved

Zachariah *(ZakarYHW)* **14:9** *And YHWH , shall be king over all the earth: in that day shall there be one YHWH , and his name* **'one'** *(one means united)*

Literally hundreds of names in Scripture have been changed resulting in the Creators true Name being hidden from public view.

- <u>Isaiah</u> – YeshaYHW – Salvation is YHW

- <u>Jeremiah</u> – YermeYHW – The Rising YHW

- <u>Joel</u> – YHW El – YHW the Strong Shepherd, Almighty

- <u>Zackariah</u> – ZakarYHW – Remember YHW

I'll stop there, but I'm sure by now you get the idea of just some of the changes that mankind has made to the Word of YHWH over time.

With all that said, I ask you - if people have been so brazenly deceptive and arrogant as to change the very Name of the Creator of the Heavens and the earth, the one who gave us life, the Almighty Shepherd, the Name above all names, the Name we are told to call upon for Salvation and for help in times of trouble – then one <u>must</u> wonder, how many other words and meanings have been changed or mistranslated in regards to the subject of women.

Matthew (*MattithYHW*) **11:29** Take My yoke upon you and learn from Me, for I am gentle and caring in heart and you will find rest for your souls.

Chapter 3

You are Not Alone - Statistics

The statistics of adult abuse and violence towards women is staggering. Though some of the statistics vary depending on who is doing the analysis and what it is being done for; and, only that which is reported can be used in statistics, in the end even the lowest numbers are beyond what most people want to admit or believe – not here, not in the United States.

Here are some numbers that will help to put things in perspective for you.

- In 70-80% of intimate partner homicides, no matter which partner was killed, the man physically abused the woman before the murder.[1]

- 85% of domestic violence victims are women.[1]

- Only approximately one-quarter of all physical assaults, one-fifth of all rapes, and one-half of all stalking perpetuated against females by intimate partners are reported to the police.[1]

- Battered women are not the only victims of abuse - it is estimated that anywhere between 3.3 million and 10 million children witness domestic violence annually.[2]

- The number one killer of African-American women ages 15 to 34 is homicide at the hands of a current or former intimate partner.[3]

- Native Americans are victims of rape or sexual assault at more than double the rate of other racial groups[4]

- 60% of all Korean immigrant women are abused

- Most perpetrators of sexual violence are men. Among acts of sexual violence committed *against women* since the age of 18, 100% of rapes, 92% of physical assaults, and 97% of stalking acts were perpetrated by men. Sexual violence *against men* is also mainly male violence: 70% of rapes, 86% of physical assaults, and 65% of stalking acts were perpetrated by men[4]

- In the past ten years, child abuse reports increased by 250%. Five hundred children die each year from abuse and at least half of all child abuse fatalities are children under one year of age. Domestic physical violence will occur at least once in two-thirds of all marriages. One out of every twenty older Americans are victims of elder abuse but only one out of ten cases of elder abuse get reported.[5]

- **In the United States, a woman is beaten every 7.4 seconds. Approximately 3-4 million women are beaten by male partners annually**[6] *(and these numbers come from only cases that are reported. It is estimated that very few cases ever get reported. The huge majority of spousal abuse victims suffer in silence.)*

These statistics vary, but all of them reveal a terrible hidden suffering. These statistics also cover only the United States – they do not include the rest of the world where in many countries the rates of abuse towards women is much, much higher and in some areas of the world rise to numbers pushing 100% where young girls growing up learn to 'expect' to be raped at some point in their lives.

Using even the smallest numbers in the statistics, there are literally uncountable women who are victims of some form of violence and/or abuse every year in the United States alone. This is a harsh reality – but it is truth. It is important to share these facts for a couple of reasons –

- To shatter the false assumptions of so many who blindly and unknowingly, believe that abuse towards women is 'rare'. In fact I have heard men try to counter what I say by repeating the above rhetoric of…."*No, that's not true, rape and abuse is rare."* Willful denial at the minimum.

- To encourage and lift the hearts of women around the world by letting you know how tragically common it really is, that you are not alone, and that more women understand what abuse feels like, than those who do not what it feels like.

Now, let's talk about emotional and psychological abuse for a moment. Statistics of these types of abuses are very difficult to obtain for obvious reasons. Let's make something clear however, one or two bouts of uncontrolled 'verbal' attack under high stress situations in a 30 year marriage does *not* constitute emotional or psychological abuse. Not one human being has lived without verbally harming someone else *unintentionally* in the heat of anger or in simple ignorance of what their words do to others.

However, unrelenting or repeated verbal attacks meant to demean, lesson, control, hurt, confuse, cause lack of confidence, or blame another person for all which goes wrong in life, *is* abuse. In the same way, continual daily insults or giving false testimony about your spouse to others in order to form a picture that will hurt them is also a form of abuse. And lastly. attempting to manipulate your spouse through lying, criticism, emotional or psychological game playing in order to maintain control of that person is also abuse.

Abuse in these forms can be very subtle in a passive/aggressive manner, very blatant, or both. And please understand, what I have mentioned only covers a very small portion of the various verbal, emotional and psychological ploys used in abuse.

Most abuse is ongoing behavior designed to crush another person's freewill spirit in order keep them controllable for the one doing the abusing, a way to make themselves appear or feel smarter, stronger etc. Instead of rising up to the be the best they can be with honor, an abuser will be lazy and simply try to knock a woman down under them.

Other times, abuse is simply a way for some religious men to exert their *self-proclaimed* superiority and/or authority over women.

Verbal abuse is just as serious as physical abuse and far more common. And yet in no way shaoe or form should any abuse be designated as 'unimportant' or 'not serious'. All abuse breaks hearts and lives to one degree or another. Imagine, if tens of millions of women are suffering physical abuse in the United States alone each year, and verbal or emotional abuse is more common – the numbers can easily reach mind-boggling heights.

Most people do not realize this. Some women even begin to tell themselves, *"Well at least he is not hitting me";* and then one day they wake up to realize they are sick, depressed, suicidal, dealing with addictions, have a lack of self-confidence, are living in darkness of mind and heart and more; and they begin to wonder what happened to their dreams, their lives and their joy.

Children who grow up in these kinds of atmospheres witnessing the abuse, are victims themselves. Some children will lean towards wanting to protect the mother, while others will lean towards appeasing the father and even join in the attack in order to protect themselves from his unbalanced dictatorship and cruelty. Children, in survival mode, can take on all kinds of behavior problems in an effort to cope with the misery, pain and destruction of abuse in households. And in one home, 3 children may form three different survival techniques. We are not clones, but all are victims of the abuse.

Male children will often (*not always*) grow up repeating what they learned from the father and abuse their girlfriends and wives. Female children will often *(not always)* grow up to repeat their mothers example and they will end up in abusive marriages. It is SO important to take into consideration what children see, hear and experience in abusive households as they learn, and repeat what they learn.

At the minimum, children in abusive household will often grow up with an unhealthy idea of what marriage, relationships and love are really all about. More than that, quite often they will grow up having little or no understanding of their own self-worth and worth to their Creator who genuinely does love them in non-cruel ways.

Now let's look at some world-wide statistics:

- Worldwide, over 60 million baby girls have been killed in forced abortions and/or killed/left to die in countries where the governing and/or religious authorities see girls and women as having far less value then boys or men.[7]

- Over 5,000 girls and women are killed by family members each year under the cruelty of so-called 'honor killings'. And most of the killings are done in very cruel ways.[8]

- More than 90 Million women suffer the torturous pain of genital mutilation in Africa each year.[9]

- In Zaria, Nigeria, more than 16% of all cases of sexually transmitted infections and diseases occur in children under the age of 5 years old![10]

These are only a small handful of statistics from a few sources, and this comes only from women who have reported abuse or are willing to speak about it. The real numbers of these abuses are far higher. It is an outrage and in no way does the genuine and TRUE love of YHWH condone these horrendous acts of violence against women or children!

But we are not done yet. There is an error in the overall concept of what violent or physical abuse is, and the idea that verbal or emotional abuse is of lesser importance as we briefly mentioned already. Studies are being done (*and have been done*) showing that those who endure many years of unrelenting verbal, emotional and/or psychological abuses have a multiplied chance of developing serious illnesses resulting in death, such as cancer, auto-immune diseases, adrenal fatigue, dementia, diabetes, arthritis, C-PTSD and more. One can simply look online for some of the results of the studies that have been done thus far. Stress 'can' kill!

So in reality, even verbal and emotional abuse is simply a precursor to violence towards the body because the body harbors all assaults. Physical pain, illness, addictions and even death are oft times a result.

For those who chose to live in denial of these atrocities towards women around the world, it is time to wake up and face reality.

And for you who have suffered or are suffering abuse at this time – allow these truths to be a loving and bold sign of strength to you that something is very wrong even beyond the borders of your own home and <u>you are not alone</u> in your suffering.

Shatan *(and abusers)* would love for you to feel like you are, as though somehow the abuse is your own fault and everyone else has perfectly happy lives – don't believe it anymore. Abuse runs rampant in many homes, societies and religions around the world. And we have only touched the tip of the iceberg on the statistics. So hang in there and let's keep going.

Chapter 4

A Common Root

Many studies done over the years have focused on the relationship of abusive households to drugs, alcohol, poverty, race, and/or education. The result of this focus has resulted in an overall picture, to those who don't know any better, that abuse towards women is mostly confined to those coming from these difficult backgrounds.

The truth is that there are no boundaries or borders when it comes to domestic violence or stranger abuse *(all types)*; abuse <u>abounds</u> in all economic levels, races, educational levels and with or without drugs and/or alcohol.

Yet, there is <u>one</u> thing that both those in poverty and those in wealth, those with higher education and those without, those of one race or those of another, most often (*but not always*) have in common: and that is...... <u>a *religious* background or mind-set that sees women overall as having lesser importance, lesser intelligence, lesser capabilities and lesser overall value than men</u>! In addition, many of these religious mind-sets teach the false belief that women in general cannot be trusted.

Even households that claim no religious preference are often found to have some sort of religious core value system in their backgrounds or families that teach this underlying and awful lie.

Rev. Dick Klaver is quoted in the Muskigon Chronicle as saying, "*One of the first things I had to face as a minister and mental-health therapist was people in the church who quoted the Bible to justify a man physically abusing a woman. I'd hear people expounding how religion validates male violence. The church has covered up (domestic) violence by encouraging women to try harder ... to behave better ... and then you won't be beaten. That is a travesty.*"

I speak truth when I say I myself have heard these very teachings in several denominations of Christianity. Please know that when I use the phrase 'Christianity', I am in no way trying to attack Christians as a whole – there are many exceptions to the rule, but truth is truth and statistics are statistics, and even without them I can testify that it is often taught in churches that when women are being abused it is somehow their own doing, their own fault, that something must be wrong with them personally and they must *try harder* to please their husbands in order to stop the abuse – just as Rev. Klaver stated in his above comment.

There are not many studies at this time on the connection between religion and domestic violence here in the United States, but according to one report in a survey of women, almost 80% of the women called themselves 'Christian'. According to the same report, up to 25% of Jewish households experienced domestic violence. Again – these numbers are coming only from those who are willing to admit it and/or report it.

So what does this mean? It means, my friends, that the vast majority of all reported domestic violence cases in the United States occurs in homes that claim some form of connection to 'Christianity'.

That means that millions of Christian men are abusing their Christian wives. Is that love? No, of course it is not. And if you have ever heard an abuser say, "I don't want to do this but I do it *because I love you*", let me tell you clearly, boldly and truthfully right now – that is not love.

Is a picture beginning to form yet that something is indeed very wrong with the 'traditional' teachings of the average Christian church *(across all denominations)* regarding women, and the impact its teachings have on secular society around the world? I hope so with all my heart because it is time to face the truth about this root of abuse and bring it out into the open.

This brings us to another devastating reality that many don't want to face regarding the number of women who endure abuse. Remembering that spousal abuse occurs across the board of both religious and secular societies, there is an additional aspect in religious homes that contributes to these horrific numbers of women being abused.

Quite often abusers are pillars in the community, respected and admired by their peers. Some abusers are even active in groups that fight abuse in order to hide their own sins within the home. Rather like the policeman who rescues the women from her abusive husband and then goes home after work and beats his own wife.

More often than not, the primary reasons for not reporting or leaving an abusive situation are:

- Fear of retaliation by the abuser

- Fear of not being believed if the spouse appears to be an upstanding citizen outside the home

- Fear of losing children and home

- Fear of judgment and humiliation in public or in a courtroom

- Being brainwashed into believing that something is wrong with them and therefore if they leave or divorce an abuser they will spend the rest of their lives alone because no one else would want them

- Fear of ability to find work and support children on their own

But Christian women, as well as women of other religions, have an additional fear that is very real to literally hundreds of millions of women around the world that keeps them bound to abusive situations and that is……Christian women, in general, have been trained to believe that they are to *'obey their husbands in all things'* no matter what, even if they are in abusive situations, and if they don't *'they will be in disobedience to god himself'*.

I personally have been witness to dozens of pastors and teachers of traditional Christianity telling women to simply endure in one way or another, that god *'hates'* divorce and if she leaves or takes her children to safety He will *'hate her too'*. I also heard one male pastor tell women on national television, that if her husband hits her she should simply respond by telling him that she loves him and that eventually it would work and the abuse would stop.

It was one of the most heartless, ignorant and shallow minded bits of public advice to women by a Christian pastor I have heard thus far.

I have sat in the pews of many churches looking around me and knowing that so many of the women sitting there with a smile on their face like proper ladies, were actually numb, dead, cold and lifeless inside because they were at that moment enduring abuse of some kind and were thus, without genuine love. And yet not one would say a word because according to many, it is God's will and/or women must endure the punishment for the first woman's sin.

So I ask….does that mean that YHWshua was lying when He said that <u>all</u> are forgiven and <u>all</u> are free in Him? We will address that a bit later along with many of the other questions we have looked at thus far. I realize that I have given you a lot of information thus far to digest and consider, but for now let's keep going with this for just a little bit more.

Let's look for just a small moment at the pornography industry. You might be asking yourself right now what that has to do with abuse. Well, it has everything to do with it.

What many don't realize is that many women who are in the pornography business have been victims of child abuse, spousal abuse or many other forms of abuse, oppression or forced labor. Many in magazines, movies, dancers in clubs, on street corners etc, were forced into the business as children, grew up with no self-worth, grew up in abusive households, ran away from abuse and ended up in the streets and much more.

So men who either are involved in, or who purchase their services, buy the magazines or even watch the late night porn movies, anyone in fact who condones these things, are only perpetuating the abuse even more and contributing to the abuse of women and children worldwide!

Statistics show that hundreds of thousands of young girls and women are kidnapped and or forced into prostitution each year worldwide. The more money put into the business, the more it thrives and the abuse occurs. And don't be deceived – this happens in the United States as well as other countries around the world.

This is but another example of how women are seen in so many societies and religions as nothing but objects of entertainment to be treated any way a man pleases – this is abuse also.

And so it continues in a seemingly endless cycle of abuse and degradation of women with the majority of abusive situations in America coming from homes with Christian beliefs or backgrounds.

Well, I have news to share with you…….

Tradition does not always equal truth. Mankind has changed the written Word of YHWH, but YHWH's Word has not changed and YHWH 'is' LOVE!

So what is the solution and what is this book really all about? This book, and in fact the entire Chayil Ishah Series, is to educate and encourage women in the truth of scripture, to shatter the lies of Shatan and mankind *(both men and women)* that have kept women in bondage and destroyed billions of lives and marriages over time both directly and indirectly.

Genesis *(1 Mosheh)* **2:23 And Adam said, This is now bone of my bones, and flesh of my flesh: she shall be called Woman** *(ishah: strong equal/fire)*, **because she was taken out of Man**

Chapter 5

The Creation of Woman

Let's get straight to the point of this chapter. If you have been seeking, you most likely are not going to want to sit around while I fill the page with nice little words in an attempt to be politically correct (*or cause no offense to anyone*). That is just not possible to do with a book such as this as there are many people in the world who do not want to see a woman filled with the strength, love and creativity that YHWH designed her to have.

If they did, they just might have to humble themselves and admit they were wrong about a few things. Many would much prefer for her to live in a dark corner feeling worthless and grateful for the crumbs on the floor. So…let's see if some new light can be shed in that corner so that you can begin to see your way out into the warm shining light of YHWH's truth and love for you.

The first myth, or rather I should say false teaching, that we are going to shatter here is the idea that women were created for the sole purpose of doing the will of men, rather like a personal possession who will be obedient to all commands of the husband and give *him* children. This idea comes from many mistranslated sources in scripture and are nothing more than the traditions of mankind.

So let's start with the creation of woman. According to the KJV in **Genesis 2:18** woman was created as a 'help-meet' for man. ***And the LORD God** (YHWH: the Strong Shepherd/Mighty One) **said, It is not good that the man should be alone; I will make him an help meet for him.'***

This translation is one of the most common. Most newer translations are not genuine translations at all but rather are the KJV or other translations, rewritten in a more modern version of English.

Since most people use one of these common versions that is where we are going to start. So exactly what IS a 'help-meet' anyway? The word 'help-meet' is an archaic word. A better way to say it is 'help-mate'. But even this translation does not even begin to describe the truth.

On the surface this verse seems to say that woman was created to be a mate and helper to her husband. That is simple enough and somewhat accurate on a shallow level. But there is much more to this word than most people know and if we leave this definition as is, much of the truth is lost. Sadly, many churches do exactly that and the masses of people who sit and listen do not realize that they're not being told the whole truth.

So, if woman was created to help man - just how is she supposed to help and with what is she supposed to help with? Most *(not all)* religions and societies including Christianity, teach that woman was created to do the will of man - whatever he says, she is to do; and many of these people use other mistranslated scripture to try and support their ideas. So for the vast majority of folks in the world, a women being the servant to her husband, obeying his commands and doing his will, is how she is supposed to help him. This however – is just wrong.

Merriam-Websters dictionary defines the word 'help' like this....*'to be of use, to change for the better, to serve food and drink.'* Many people teach only the final portion of this modern English definition which results in the traditional idea of a woman in the kitchen. A lie has become tradition and is believed as truth by billions.

Now, there is nothing wrong with cooking and in fact I love making healthy, fun and tasty meals for my husband, because I love him and wish him to be healthy and strong so that he can lead a long and healthy life together with me. But there is a huge difference between serving others out of genuine love, as both men and women should do for each other; and, the idea that woman was created for the sole purpose of serving men and obeying his will. This is just wrong according to properly translated scripture.

The Hebrew word for help is 'ezer' and it means *'to aid or assist' (Note there is no mention of serving food and drink here).* It is derived from an ancient root word, 'azar' which means *'to surround, to protect and to aid'.* Even here we can begin to see the difference, but let's keep looking.

In the ancient pictographs, each letter (*picture*) had a meaning of its own. Two and three letters (*or pictures*) were placed together to make a root word. The meanings of each letter (*or picture*) combined creates a fuller, deeper, and broader meaning as one word.

As an example, the word El *(properly AL)* in the pictographs is a picture of an ox-head (*the aleph - which means strength*) and a shepherd's staff (*the lamad -which represents a shepherd, or more directly, the authority of a shepherd or to point towards something*) and it looks like this ᒐᗄ When you combine these two pictographs you get the meaning of 'a Strong Shepherd', or 'Almighty'. There are deeper meanings but I'm sure you get the point here.

So let's get back to the word 'azar'. It contains two root words. One means *'strong and bold'* and the other means *'to spread out over a large area'*. The true and most correct definition of the word used in Scripture *(as a whole and full meaning) is 'to be strong and bold, covering a large area, to surround, aid and assist'*.

Now how different is that from the modern interpretation of *'to serve food and drink'*. An eye opening, amazing and wonderful difference, don't you think?

We see a similar example in yet another scripture. It is found in **Titus 2:5.** In this scripture we see that the first things mentioned are being safe and sound in the mind and morally clean (*Which is not the same as being self-righteous by the way*); the third thing mentioned is 'housekeeper' and this is the example we are going to look at. We viewed it briefly already but let's look a little closer now. The word housekeeper is the traditionally taught translation of the Greek word 'oikorous'.

Most people have been taught that this means *'one who cleans the home'*. Many people take this even further using Strong's interpretation by saying that a women is supposed to remain in the home 24/7.

As we all know, it is good to keep our homes clean and take care of what YHWH has given us, and what has been worked for; but, *'to clean house'* is a grossly <u>incorrect</u> definition of the word 'oikorous'. In fact the word oikorous has <u>nothing</u> to do with cleaning house.

The first half of the word is <u>'oikos'</u> which means *'home, house, dwelling'*. This part was translated correctly. The second half of the word is 'ouros' and is usually translated as 'keeper' and thus we get 'housekeeper'. Interestingly some bible dictionaries don't even give a definition for the second half of this word.

Here is truth.... 'ouros' means *to keep safe, to guard, to watch over and protect.*

Common sense dictates that in order to be a good guardian of dwellings and people, a guard must be strong, capable, wise and courageous in many areas; and this is what a Chayil Ishah is and that is what Chayil Ishah means…..

...a Strong and Valiant Woman

My purpose is not to direct your individual lives nor attempt to direct your marriages – we are unique individuals and each and every woman on the Earth is <u>one of a kind</u> – we are not clones. So please let us not take this to the opposite extreme and feel as if no woman should want to be a house cleaner or a stay at home Mom. Again – it is the idea of teaching all women, that all women, are to love doing the same thing – *IE:Stay at home and clean house.*

Genesis 1:27-28 **So God** *(YHWH)* **created man** *(humans/mankind)* **in his own image, in the image of God** *(YHWH)* **created he him; male and female created he them. And God** *(YHWH)* **blessed** <u>them</u>**, and God** *(YHWH)* **said to** <u>them</u>**, Be fruitful, and multiply, and replenish the earth, and subdue it: and have dominion over the fish of the sea, and over the fowl of the air, and over every living thing that moves upon the earth.**

YHWH gave Adam <u>and</u> Eve *(ChWH – to live/give life)* the job of reproducing, filling the earth, being fruitful (*which is more than just producing offspring as YHW the Savior often spoke of spiritual fruit*), having dominion over and caring for all living things upon the earth that YHWH created and they were to do this as 'one' – united together.

Nowhere in the creation of woman does YHWH dictate that the woman was to remain in the home and do nothing but the will of man - nowhere does it say that.

So what are women supposed to help with? We are to help our husbands do YH's will - as a companion, a strong and valiant partner; and, a friend. Man and woman were to become one and work together caring for each other and the creations of YHWH.

Scripture does <u>not</u> say that the man is supposed to go out and conquer the world while the woman stays in the home and does laundry.

Please understand – if you are blessed with a heart that desires to remain in the home, caring for it and raising children – that is a beautiful thing and it is a blessing. That is our individual choice and/or necessity of circumstance. But to teach that all women are to be exactly the same and have the same talents and desires of heart and remain in the home is just wrong.

Does this mean that a woman should suddenly dismiss the needs of her family and run off in pursuit of selfish gain or desire? No, of course not – becoming one means working together with your husband, and he with you, which means taking each other's needs into consideration – not to overtake, over power, or *rule over* each other.

But it does mean that if you have been gifted with a desire to go to school, be a doctor, raise cattle or own a book store, YHWH never dictated that you cannot pursue those desires of heart. In fact, it is YHWH who gives us talents to use for good purpose. To prevent a woman from pursuing her heart's desires in this way, is to prevent her from using the gifts that YHWH gave to her. It is to interfere in YHWH's will for her life!

Our Creator also saw that man was lonely and so created woman, who also would be a good companion and friend because He saw that man was simply not 'whole' without her. .

According to properly translated scripture, men and women are to become one, that is two joining together, <u>not</u> one absorbing, overshadowing or having dominion over the other.

<u>Genesis 2:24</u> - Therefore shall a man leave his father and his mother, and shall cleave *(to adhere to another person)* **his wife: and they shall be one** *(united as one)* **flesh.**

Woman was created to be a companion to the man, to complete him because he was not whole or properly functional without her, and to help him to the will of YHWH which is honoring Him and caring for each other and His creations on this Earth.

<u>Ephesians 5:28</u> - So ought men to love their wives as their own bodies. He that loves his wife loves himself.

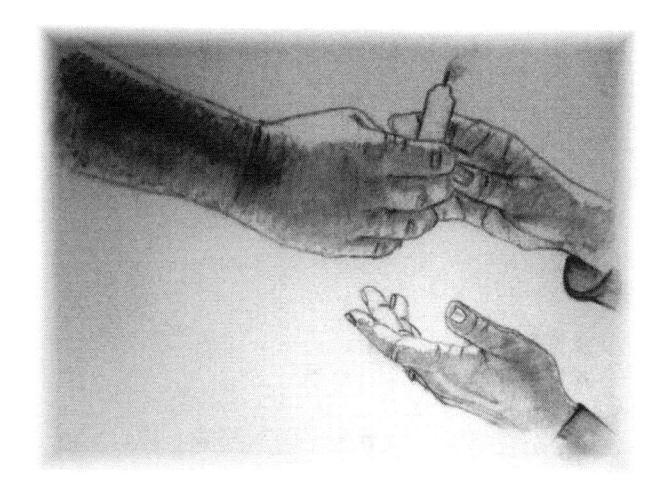

Psalms 18:28 For you will light my candle: YHWH my Elohym will enlighten *(light up)* my darkness.

Chapter 6

Exposing the Lie with the Light of Truth

There is a common belief in the world, in many religions and secular societies, that all women are gullible, easily deceived and less intelligent than men in general. There is also a very common belief in many religions and societies that women both in-general and individually are personally responsible for all the evil or pain in the world.

So where did this idea come from ?

I'm going to show you here and now, where most of it comes from, how and why; and then what the truth really is. It is time to be set free from the lying tongues, the bias and the condemnation and allow the Light of Truth to show you the Way out of the darkness.

Let's start with the most common religious story about the 'fall' of mankind which occurred in the garden. Paraphrased and summarized it goes something like this in most people's minds:

- A 'snake' approached the woman and convinced her to take a bite of an 'apple'. So the woman, being gullible and/or 'evil', took the apple from the snake, ate a bite of it and then handed it to Adam. Adam took the apple from the woman and also took a bite. Just a short while later, 'God' came looking for them. When god asked what happened, the woman confessed that she had been deceived by the snake. When 'God' asked the man what happened he told god it was the woman's fault for giving it to him. He then reminded god that He (*God*) was the one who gave the woman to him. Basically dumping off all blame of the man's personal choice onto both the woman and 'God'. So 'God' got mad, and cursed the woman with terrible pain during child birth and declared a new 'law' that from that point forward that the husband would <u>'rule over'</u> the wife. He then also cursed the ground, cursed the snake and kicked the man and woman out of the garden.

So according to most people who believe that, the entire reason that the man was kicked out of the garden was the woman's fault and the man was basically innocent in the entire event.

This version also makes it appear as though YHWH is an angry vengeful being towards those who make innocent or uninformed errors – no grace, no mercy, no compassion and no understanding. That in itself is a terrible misconception about YHWH however, that story is for another book. Let's remain focused on the subject at hand for now.

From there individual people and religions have simply added their own twists depending on their personal motivations such as: man ruling over woman was her punishment, man needs to rule over woman because she is too gullible to make good choices on her own, man needs to control woman because she is evil or untrustworthy – the list goes on and on.

What you just read of course is tradition, not truth, and it stems from those who refuse to take responsibility for their own actions and choose instead to blame others – in this case, specifically women.

YHWH's Word did not change – It was mankind that changed YHWH's written Word.

One of the biggest instigators in the 'Modern' Christian Church of these false ideas was a man by the name of Tertullian who lived in 155-245 (AD).

Robert Wilken writes: "*In spite of his lapse from the Church, Tertullian exercised a great influence on the Latin Fathers who were to follow him. As the initiator of ecclesiastical Latin, he was instrumental in shaping the vocabulary and thought of Western Christianity for the next 1,000 years."*[16]

Tertullian said, while speaking directly to the women in a crowd, ..."*And do you not know that you are each an Eve? The sentence of God on this sex of yours lives in this age: the guilt must of necessity live too. You are the devil's gateway: you are the un-sealer of that forbidden tree: you are the first deserter of the divine law: you are she who persuaded him whom the devil was not valiant enough to attack. You destroyed so easily God's image, man. On account of your desert — that is, death— even the Son of God had to die.*[17]

While Tertullian is not wholly responsible for this deception, and it started in the garden with Adam, he did indeed have a great influence on the Roman Catholic Church which is the foundation of most modern day Christian denominations and, was being formed through the Roman Empire's political agenda's during those times. With the spread of Christianity around the world, these ideas have permeated otherwise equal gender societies all over the world.

The devastating effect of this is that hundreds of millions, if not billions, of people around the world over time have come to believe that women are inferior beings who are unable to think well, untrustworthy and even 'evil'; and therefore men must *rule over* them like property. It is also extremely sobering and devastating to face the fact that many women have come to believe this, too, simply because it is drilled into their hearts and minds repeatedly from birth through individuals, cultures, societies and religions – including many denominations of Christianity which is what we are addressing here.

The blame game that started in the garden has continued throughout history and remains intact today. It's time to put a stop to it with the beautiful <u>truth</u> of YHWH's love for both His sons <u>and</u> daughters.

Some of the logical questions that you might be thinking right now are:

- Carry the guilt? I thought YHWshua forgives our sins.

- Carry the guilt? I thought Scripture said that a child was not responsible for a parent's sin and vice-versa; So how can anyone say I am responsible for, or must pay the price for a woman who lived thousands of years ago?

- So if a man makes a poor choice in life and it causes him a problem, it is somehow my fault because my great,

great, great, great, great ancestor was deceived?

- So if the Spirit of YHWH fills a woman – then, um, what does that mean? That because He is in a woman the Spirit becomes weakened? Diminished? Untrustworthy? Just how does that work?

- Or is it that the Spirit of YHWH simply cannot be in a woman. If that is the case then YHWshua must have lied.

Again, I hope you are seeing that something is amiss, something is not making logical sense, something is not lining up.

We are to fight evil with good so **let's put this old lie to the grave permanently by speaking truth!**

Here is truth: The word commonly translated as 'serpent' or 'snake' in scripture is NChSh (*nachash*). It means 'to whisper' or 'the whisperer' – 'like the hissing sound of a snake'.

So right at the get-go we find that there was no physical snake but rather a whispering being who was out to deceive and cause destruction and harm, to steal the joy and beauty of not only the union of the two people but also creation itself.

John *(YHWchanon)* 10:10 The thief only comes to steal, kill and destroy. I came that they may have life and may have it abundantly!

The second key word to look at is the word 'tree'. The original word is 'ETs'. This word can mean 'tree' in the right context, however, as with most ancient words and YHWH's Word especially, there are many levels of meaning and depths to understanding not only each word but each letter, rather like what we call 'homonyms'[18] in the English language.

The word 'ETs', then, is also related to the word 'counsel'. The ancients saw the leaders of a tribe rather like strong trees and when they gathered together for 'counsel' it was related to a grove, or forest, of trees.

Are you beginning to see the 'whispering counsel' that is like the poison of a snake?

Okay, the last word we are going to look at right now is the word 'fruit'. Over time the majority of the world has been taught that the 'fruit' was an apple. Let's give the poor apple some credit here. It is a known and scientific fact that apples are of supreme nutritional value. You know that old saying "An apple a day keeps the doctor away"? Well, apples really are an amazing fruit. They are packed full of goodness for the body.

Do we really think that something YHWH created for our good health would be something that He told us not to eat? That just does not make sense, does it?

Many churches simply teach that the fruit was unknown. But the word often translated as 'fruit' is PRY *(pery)*. This word means not only fruit but, also a 'reward' as in the fruits of one's labor, or the logical consequence of one's actions; rather like the reward of someone's work or decision. So what actually happened *(paraphrase*d), is that the woman was deceived by the whispering/counsel and received his words into her mind/heart.

But what was the deception? What was the counsel that she listened to and chose to believe? The whisperer was telling her that basically, she did not need to listen to YHWH, that she did not need His counsel or His guidance – saying, "Surely, you will not die", as though it was YHWH who had not spoken the truth.

The woman, not fully understanding the boundaries of safety YHWH had set forth and the instructions to not take the 'fruit' etc, as she was indeed the newer creature – took it.

Then what happened? She passed that along to the man. Scripture does not say that man was deceived – in fact he was not. The man, unlike the women, made a willful and purposeful choice to disobey YHWH as He has had many a conversation with YHWH before the woman was created. The man was right there. He knew that YHWH had said if they took of the counsel from the whisperer that they would die. But Adam said nothing to the woman and instead let her take of it, saw that she didn't die physically, and chose of his own free will to also take of it when she then offered it to him..

YHWH gives each and every person freewill choice just like we discussed at the beginning of this book; both the woman <u>and</u> the man chose of their own freewill not only to disobey YHWH, but also to ignore each other – each of them was only thinking about themselves.

The woman should have said to the whisperer, "Wait, I want to ask YHWH about this." or "Wait, my husband spoke with YHWH directly about this earlier. I would like to see what he says before making my decision." But instead pride got in her way and she decided she didn't need to consult YHWH first – basically making decisions without all the facts for prideful or impatient reasons.

Now don't get me wrong, we are given freewill choice and we make dozens, if not hundreds, of decisions in that freewill choice every day of our lives and we need to do that. YHWH gave each of us reasoning and learning skills that we are to make use of in wisdom. However, as a child ignores a parent's guiding, rules or advice because of a lack of respect or a belief that he or she is as wise or knowledgeable as the parent, so the woman and the man also disregarded the Father YHWH in the same way.

The man should have said, "Wait woman, I love you and I don't want you to die. Don't believe the whisperer. Everything YHWH has told us so far has been true. Let us talk to Him first. Let us investigate his claim before you make this decision." He should have stepped up to the plate and protected the woman… in love for her and in trust in YHWH.

He could have, and should have, said "Wait – don't do it. Let's talk about this first", because He had heard firsthand from YHWH about receiving counsel from the whisperer, the deceiver. But he did not, instead he chose to totally ignore Him, and on top of that he chose to allow the woman's life to be at risk and waited in silence to see what would happen and then he trusted his own judgment and his own understanding.

At the very least, if she had already been deceived, if she had already chosen to ignore the opportunity to speak with YHWH or her husband, the man could have easily refused to join her. But again – he did not. He made his own choices and they were the wrong ones.

However, instead of taking responsibility for his own actions – he simply tried to claim innocence by placing the entire blame onto the woman.

Scripture tells us that pride came before the fall and indeed it did. Shatan was prideful and it caused him to fall from the grace of YHWH. He then went after the man <u>and</u> woman by going through the woman and tempting her with her own pride; and in turn she tempted the man with his own pride. <u>Both</u> fell under their own pride.

<u>Proverbs 16:18</u> - Pride goes before destruction and arrogance before a fall.

<u>1 Tim. 3:6</u> - He must not be a new convert, lest falling into arrogance he fall into the same trap of pride as Shatan did.

In the case of Adam and Eve (ChWH), it was the woman who was the newer creation, similar to that of being a newer believer, and therefore she was more susceptible to pride.

When YHWH asked the woman what happened, she admitted honestly about being deceived. When YHWH asked the man what happened, he basically blamed both the woman and YHWH Himself saying 'You' are the one who gave 'her' to me – 'she' made me take it. This was the first move in the 'Blame Game'.

I have often wondered if things would have turned out differently if the woman would have said, "I am so sorry Father. And I am so sorry husband. I should have come to you and talked to you about this because I am here to help you do YHWH's will and instead I sought after my own goals for selfish reasons."

And, if the man would have said, "I am so sorry Father. And I am so sorry wife. I did not love you enough to intervene and stop the whisperer from deceiving you and causing you and I harm. I did not step forward in courage and protect you as I should have done. Will you forgive me?"

Ephesians 4:32 And be ye kind one to another, tenderhearted, forgiving one another, even as YHWH for the Messiah's sake has forgiven you.

Oh, how far honestly and genuine love might have gone! But instead, here we are, thousands of years later; and, the blame game which is no game, continues to be taught and exercised by many resulting in the ultimate abuse of millions upon millions of wives and women in general.

Have you ever wondered why Adam said *'the woman you gave to me'* when he was dodging the responsibility of his actions? It is easy to see if one simply puts it in modern form. Imagine a parent saying to a child, "Johnny, you know I told you not to drink anymore soda, why did you drink it anyway?" And the child responds, "It was Freddie's fault, he gave it to me. Besides, <u>you are the one</u> who introduced us at the picnic last week."

A parent would <u>immediately</u> realize that the child was not only trying to lay the blame on another child instead of being honest about his own choices, but also trying to shirk his responsibility by blaming the parent for introducing them. Can you see the shadow of intention in Adam's response now?

Again – I must pause and say, my point is not to reverse the blame game and start pointing to the man, but rather to expose the lies, and the root of much abuse, mistrust and blame dumping. It must stop and both men and women ought begin to live in the freedom and love of YHWH together as one beautiful partnership. Woman is not responsible for man's choices and, man is not responsible for woman's choices.

<u>Deuteronomy 23:16</u> The fathers shall not be cast out for the children, neither shall the children be cast out for the fathers, every man shall be cast out for his own sin.

Matthew *(MatithYHW)* **12:34** says that each one of us is judged by our own words. That means we are responsible for our own thoughts, our own words and our own actions. It is time to stop the blame game.

Time and time again we read in scripture that YHWH is a forgiving, merciful and loving Creator. He forgives us the things we have done wrong, the hurts we have caused others, and the insult we have directed towards Him. Why is it so difficult for men to realize that woman is 'not' to be blamed and belittled for everything that goes wrong in life?

Leviticus 19:18 Leviticus 19:18 You shall not avenge, nor bear any grudge against the children of your people, but you shall love your neighbor as yourself: I am YHWH.

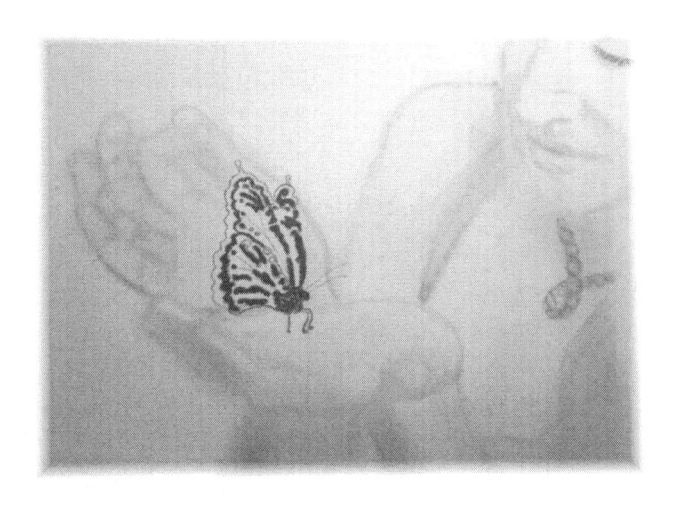

Colosians 3:19 Husbands, love your wives and do <u>not</u> be harsh with them.

Chapter 7

A Touch Like Silk

Now that we have covered the traditional teachings of the 'Rule of Genesis' and the common thread of the blame game – let's look at the truth of properly translated scripture and see what YHWH <u>really </u>says about this.

The Word of YHWH has not changed - mankind has changed the written Word.

YHWH's Word, when properly translated clearly shows that women are no more and no less loved and valued than men; yet literally billions of men over time have come to believe it is their inherent right to abuse and/or control women, and billions of women over time have been told the abuse they endure is their own fault, simply because they are a woman. How did this horrible state of misery come to be?

We saw in the last chapter that it began with the refusal of Adam to take responsibility for his own actions. I have personally heard in modern church services things like, "The woman acted out of gullibility, selfishness and had less natural ability to comprehend things; while the man acted only out of his heart on innocence to please her. Therefore the man must take charge over the woman because women simply do not have the ability to understand as well as men."

So this old worn out, false and corrupted teaching is still very present in the teachings of Christian churches. It is appalling to hear such ignorance taught and what is even more frightening is that so many still simply accept whatever a pastor says without questioning anything.

Women especially have been taught to not speak up or question anything other than asking her husband. Now let me ask you, in a male dominated, abusive or controlling household – do we really think she will get an honest, logical, balanced or genuinely discerning answer?

Scripture however, tells us the opposite. Scripture tells us to test all things to see if it is truly of the Spirit of YHWH or not. So let's honor that and do some more digging and put a stop to these atrocities towards women.

Let's look at one last piece of this old root and in doing so, hopefully and prayerfully the truth will release you into the Light of Truth and freedom from abuse; and, set you on a journey to healing, wholeness and joy!!

The bottom line is that most people, both men and women, have been taught that 'god' said man is supposed to rule over women *(husbands are to rule over wives)*. Well, maybe the god that they worship did say that. But YHWH did not! Let's do it then, we will look at a couple of scriptures used to teach the domination of women and then we will dig and find out what is really being said in them.

<u>Genesis 3:16</u> 'To the woman he said, "I will greatly multiply your sorrow and your conception; in sorrow you shall bring forth children; and your desire shall be to your husband, and he shall <u>rule over</u> thee".

It is commonly taught that 'god' was cursing and punishing the woman for being deceived.

Most religious people back up this teaching by quoting another scripture story found in **Esther 1:22.**

<u>Esther 1:22</u> "For he sent letters into all the king's provinces, into every province according to the writing thereof, and to every people after their language, that <u>every man should bear rule in his own house</u>, and that it should be published according to the language of <u>every</u> people."

These are the two main scriptures people use to try and prove that god wanted men to *rule over* women. We find other scriptures later speaking of wives being told to submit to their husbands in all things also. But those we will address later. Let's focus on these for now as these are the root of so many women suffering and enduring abuse at the hands of men who ignorantly believe they have some sort of god-given right to do so.

Now I don't know about you but I had questions. Things like…..

- If god cursed women with pain during child birth – then what about women who are unable to have children? Why would he punish only *some* women in this way? I thought He was a fair judge of people?

- So how does this work? When a woman is single, making her own decisions, working, owning her own home and taking care of herself – then what? – As soon as she gets married she suddenly becomes stupid and unable to make decisions for herself and a man must do it for her?

- So according to the bible women are inherently untrustworthy? Wait, wait, wait…..if women are inherently untrustworthy then why was it that YHWshua chose a woman to be the first to see Him after He rose and then entrusted her with the first and most important message of His resurrection to go and share with the men? And then He then chastised the men later for not believing her when she did tell them!

There are many more questions obviously, and there are many more instances in scripture where YHWH chose a woman to do some very important things - but these will give you an idea of how this just doesn't make sense, not to mention insulting millions of women of valor and intelligence.

In addition, brilliant women over the centuries have been prevented from contributing to the health, wellness and good of the human race because so many have been prevented from attending school or working, at the orders of their husbands who keep them bound within their homes scrubbing floors under the guise of religion. And these are the easier things to mention. As anyone who has ever been abused knows, there are uncountable things that have occurred in the name of religion and men ruling over women.

So....what does the Word really say? What did He really say to the woman and the man, and what happened in Esther that caused a king to make a law about it?

Let's start with *'the desire of the woman to be towards her husband'*. Most of Christianity teaches that it means a woman's only, or biggest, desire should be to please her husband.

Now, we all know that we are to love each other in the same way that YHWshua loves us and in the same way we love ourselves. We are also supposed to hold each other in a higher regard than ourselves and we are to serve each other just as He came and served us. But that works both ways; and, it does not take into account the times when a woman has been so taken advantage of that she not only looses her identity, but may become ill and desperately needs to focus on herself for healing etc.

Now it is very natural and YHWH given that when we love someone, we want to please and honor them. That is <u>not</u> a question here. Husbands and wives, when they truly love each other will go out of their way to do things for each other to cause them joy or happiness – that is a joy of love.

However, it is often taught that a woman should have <u>no other</u> desire in life than to work at pleasing her husband. As though if she had a heart's desire to attend school or go to work there must be something wrong with her.

We need to get serious and blunt here, this is not a time to beat around the bush - when speaking of abusive situations, it is nearly impossible for a woman to please her husband no matter how hard she tries. Abusive husbands are rarely, if ever, happy or satisfied with a wife's efforts or love.

So for an abused woman, she becomes engrossed with trying to run and fret in an impossible attempt to please someone who is not genuinely looking to be pleased and this truly can cause her great pain in addition to mental, emotional and physical exhaustion to say the <u>very least</u>, because nothing she does will <u>ever</u> be good enough in the abusers eyes or will ever please her spouse.

We must remember that abuse is used to try and control, lesson or belittle others. So matter how hard a woman tries, if she is married to an abuser, the abuser will make sure she knows it was not good enough.

The word in this scripture translated as 'desire' is TShWQH. There are many root words in this one word. Remember that single pictographs and/or two and three letter roots words are placed together to form broader concepts and meanings. All put together, the meaning of this word is rather like an overflowing river, to drink from a river of living water, success and the mark of something – and more. The idea is that the woman's life and love will overflow onto her husband like that of living waters, to pour out her love onto him and is not just a self-centered way of life.

And the last and most important word we need to look at is the word translated as simply 'rule over' by most people. This is the one that has caused the destruction of so many lives over the centuries as cruelty sets in and harsh rule takes over in marriages and even going down the line with dating, casual acquaintance and the general idea of men ruling over women.

Before we go there however, please know that the word 'over' never even existed in the scriptures. It is a word that was, and continues to be, added by those who desire it to be there. I will repeat that for clarity – the word 'over', as in 'rule over' – NEVER existed in the original writings – it was added.

We are warned in Revelations of the dangers of adding to or taking from His original word!

Now let's look at the word rule. The word is MShL *(mashal)*. The <u>same</u> word means 'proverb' when pronounced slightly differently. One of the root words found in MShL is MSh. It means having a soft touch like silk. The last letter, 'L', is represented by a shepherd's staff in pictographs and it means *the authority of a shepherd, towards something.*

All of this put together means that the husband is supposed to watch out for the woman, being like a good shepherd with a *touch like silk*. He is to also be like a proverb, using wisdom to guide and direct the wife rather like a shepherd would lead a sheep to green pastures, to water, <u>to safety</u>.

If one pictures how a loving protective shepherd would behave, that is the meaning of this word. A proverb is a wise saying either written or spoken that helps to keep a person on a safe and right path in life. They are 'rules' to live by. Proverbs are loving direction and when given in love and wisdom, a person desires to heed them.

In the same way, a husband who shows true love and wisdom towards the wife will be a loving and SAFE beacon for her to look to and lean on, like a guiding light in the dark times.

As mentioned earlier, the wife should have talked it over with her husband or with YHWH before making the decision but she did not.

And the husband should have watched out for and protected the wife by intervening and saying let's talk about this first, or something to that effect. But he did not.

YHWH was not punishing the woman, nor telling the woman that she was incapable, nor does His written Word say that man is supposed to have dominion over, or rule over his wife. Rather in proper translation it states that the husband should be gentle, loving and protective and that he should exemplify what a proverb is, what a wise shepherd is – caring for his wife. It says that the wife should allow her love and life to overflow towards the husband. They needed to have this kind of a relationship because from that point forward the world would be full of difficulties that would cause mothers to worry and have sorrow in the raising of her children.

Regarding capabilities, nowhere in this incident does YHWH say that the purpose of the woman's creation changed, or got cut back, or restricted. Her purpose never changed. When we go through **Proverbs 31** among other accounts of women in scripture in future books, we will see that very clearly.

It is a lie to teach that men are supposed to 'rule over' women. It is simply a blatant lie according to YHWH's Word when properly translated and understood.

The Backup to the Lie

Now let's skip over to Esther and see what that one is all about. Pastors and priests and laymen for centuries have said that **Esther** is simply a repeat, an upholding, a confirmation of the idea that man is supposed to rule over a woman. But this also is a false.

At the time of Esther, put simply, the kingdom was ruled by a Persian King. He was attempting to rally the support of several of the surrounding kingdoms and basically threw a big bash inviting all of the rulers of those kingdoms. Towards the end of the events which lasted for a couple of weeks, the king was very drunk and ordered that his wife, Queen Vashti (*Wshti*) be brought out to stand before all the people so they could see how beautiful she was.

At the time she was having her own party with the women and refused the king's order. Many have guessed at why she did this…some have demonized her and others have defended her. The truth is that Scripture doesn't tell us exactly why, though her name does give us a clue.

Root words in her name when properly spelled *(WShTY – pronounced Oo-shti)* and the individual meanings of the letters tell us that her works may well have been because of drunkenness also. With this additional understanding it can easily been seen that both the king and the queen were drunk.

We know that often when a person is drunk they will say or do things that they normally would not. So, Vashti should neither be demonized nor defended as we don't have all the facts of her mindset at the time of her refusal.

None the less she did refuse and when she did, the king became angry because he was trying to show off his power and what he 'owned' and her refusal embarrassed him in front of everyone he was trying to impress. So, he asked his Persian advisers *(who did not know, love or honor YHWH – just as the King did not either)* what he should do about it. They responded by saying, "If word gets out that the queen disobeyed you, then all the men in the kingdom will start having trouble with their wives. So you should banish her permanently and make a law that says that the men are the rulers of their homes."

So the king agreed and signed the order and sent a new Persian law out to all the provinces in the kingdom stating that men should be the ruler in the houses.

It needs to be noted that if this king knew or honored YHWH, or if his advisors did, then there would be no need to make a law, because YHWH's MShL already existed and this event would have not taken place if both the king and queen were honoring a loving marriage.

After the king sobered up, he thought about his queen and became sad. He missed her. His advisers then suggested that he find a new queen. So they sent men out, going around the kingdom and collecting beautiful young virgins to take the queen's place. The king agreed and ultimately Esther was chosen as the new queen.

Now there is much more to the story of Esther which we will look at a different time, but for this book and the subject of abuse, let's focus on this <u>new</u> rule of marriage and man dominating, controlling, ruling over, wives and how it has played such a vital part in the control and abuse of women over the centuries.

Let's break this down and look at it with some clarity for a refreshing change.

- This was a king who did not honor YHWH and cared not for YHWH's people at the time he laid down this 'new law' about husbands 'ruling' in the home.
- He was throwing a party to show off all of his possessions.
- He was drunk.
- He was angry.
- His advisers came up with the idea of a new law.
- In his drunken anger he agreed
- Persian law could not be revoked.

This series of events had nothing to do with YHWH's order that the wife overflow her attention and love to her husband and that the husband should watch over the wife with the idea of being a living proverb, a wise and gentle leader and protector to the wife.

In fact, the word translated in Esther as 'rule' is not the same word used in the first story at all. Remember that word was MShL. The word in Esther is SRR (sarar). Sarar means to turn someone from the right direction to the wrong direction, to make oneself a prince, to rule like a prince, to 'take' dominion or authority over.

This was not the law or decree of YHWH, it was a new law created by a drunk, angry Persian king. Yet because of the corruption and bias of the male translators through the ages, the two different words, that have two VERY different meanings - have both been translated as simply 'rule' leaving the vast majority of those reading scripture in English to believe they mean the same thing.

They absolutely do NOT. Do not be deceived any longer. Husbands are NOT supposed to rule over their wives, control their wives every move or treat their wives as anything but the helpful, beautiful, intelligent, loving beings that they are!

Abuse and control through ruling over women is not something that YHWH said should happen and nowhere in correctly translated scripture does He condone such behavior towards his daughters *(or his sons)*.

In fact we find repeatedly that He tells husbands to treat their wives with love, honor, gentleness and faithfulness.

Malachi 2:13-15 And this have you done again, covering the altar of YHWH with tears, with weeping, and with crying out, insomuch that he regards not the offering any more, or receives it with good will at your hand. Yet you say, Wherefore? Because YHWH has been witness between you and the wife of your youth, against whom you have dealt treacherously: yet is she your companion, and the wife of your covenant. And did not he make one? Yet had he the residue of the spirit. And wherefore one? That he might seek a godly seed. Therefore take heed to your spirit, and let none deal treacherously against the wife of his youth.

In simply words, the above scripture is saying that tears are shed by the men because YHWH is ignoring their offers and prayers. When they ask YHWH 'why' He is ignoring them, He says quite clearly it is because He has seen how they treat their wives. And then admonishes the men to not dare to treat their wives badly.

VERY sadly, most people use this same scripture to try and tell women they are not to divorce their abusive husbands. In reality – YHWH is speaking to the men, not the women; and, the word doesn't just mean divorce, it means to push away, to keep at a distance. Abuse and indifference does just that – pushes a woman away because no women in her right mind 'desires' to be abused, instead, she will pull her heart back to herself because the hands of untrustworthy abusers are not where she desires her heart to be.

We are also told in scripture that husbands are to love their wives so that their prayers will not be hindered. Abuse is not love. And yet the woman is often blamed still for the husbands prayers not being answered instead of looking at their own behavior.

.

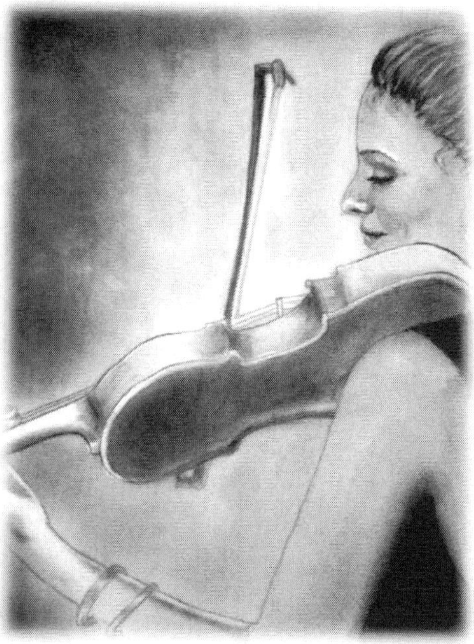

Chapter 8

Healing the Broken Hearted

Isaiah (YeshaYHW) 61:1-3 The Spirit of the master (*Adoni*) YHWH is upon me; because YHWH has anointed me to preach good tidings to the meek *(depressed);* he has sent me to bind up the brokenhearted, to proclaim liberty to the captives, and the opening of the prison to them that are bound;

Luke 4:18 "The Spirit of YHWH is upon me, because he has anointed me to preach good news to the poor; he has sent me to heal the brokenhearted, to preach deliverance to the captives, and recovering of sight to the blind, to set at liberty them that are bruised,

YHWshua came to heal the broken hearted, to bind wounds, to open the eyes to the spiritually blind. He is the great healer and His healing is done with love.

Each woman is a unique creation, each has had her own life experiences and has her own individual dreams and hopes and pain in life. And while billions of women have been abused over time, each has her own unique experience with, and within, that abuse. Therefore each woman goes through the healing process a little differently. We are not clones. But healing can and will come if you seek it with all your heart and are ready to work for it and be finally be free.

He will show you the perfect path for you as a unique individual to achieve that healing in your life; and He does it all in His amazing and perfect love.

When we look in Scripture, we see that even when he healed the physically blind, He did it in different ways for each person. On one was a mixture of mud, on another He simply placed His hands over the man's eye and more. We are not all healed in the exact same way and in the exact same timing – but the beautiful light and hope of truth is that healing <u>can</u> come.

There is also a tendency in an abusive relationship for the woman to believe that she will be healed, she will be happy, she will be okay – if only the husband would change. The truth is that we cannot force change onto another human being, we were all designed with freewill choice in life. It is also truth to say the on a woman's end, no one can stop you from seeking and leaning on YHWH either.

No matter what kinds of choices other people in your life make; you, as a woman, have the absolute right in YHWH by the freewill given to us in creation, to seek healing, peace, strength and joy in life no matter what anyone else does.

And when we seek with all our hearts and do not give up – it can be found.

Even though each woman's experience may be very different, pain is universal. Every form of abuse, every degree of it, is devastating and harmful, crushing the hearts of women all over the world. But the wonderful thing about YHWH is that He knows each woman's heart personally and intimately. He knows exactly what we need to be healed and how that healing needs to come both in practical terms and in timing.

His love is so great that it can penetrate and sooth the deepest of wounds to the soul, and I can give testament to that truth. The meaning of His genuine word *(versus corrupted and manipulated biased translations)* reveals an amazing Creator who is pure love: **John 4:8.**

Time and time again in Scripture we see the healing love of YHWshua reaching out to those who are hurting and in need, quite the contrast from so many of the teachings about woman today.

- **Matt. 9** – A woman who had an illness related to her cycle reached out and touched Him and He healed her in love. At the time it was against the law for her as a woman with 'blood' to touch a priest or enter a temple.

- **Matt 15** – A woman called out to Him to help her daughter who was ill. <u>He healed her in love</u>.
- **Matt 26** – A woman full of sins came to Him in love to anoint His head with oil in a symbolic act of both His Kingship and in her gratitude and love for Him. When the self-righteous in the gathering chastised her for that, <u>He defended her saying 'leave her alone. She is doing this in love, what have YOU done for me</u>?'
- **Luke 13** – While teaching in a temple, He saw a woman who was crippled and had been for many years. <u>He healed her right then.</u> The arrogant rulers of the temple became angry because it was a manmade law that people were not to be healed on a Sabbath – they considered it work. <u>But YHW healed the woman in love anyway</u>.
- **John 4** – YHWshua stopped to speak with a lone woman at a water-well. Being illegal for him to speak with her alone, He spoke with her anyway. *(By this time MANY manmade laws had been created 'against' women as the blame game and hypocrisy continued)* He had an <u>intelligent conversation</u> with her and explained to her in His way, who He was. She then went off and told others and because of her, many came

to know Him. <u>He took the time and the love to spend with her one on one even though it was against the law</u>.

- **John 8** – The authorities brought a woman to Him and tried to trick Him asking what to do with her because she was 'caught' in adultery. Their <u>manmade</u> laws allowed them to stone her for it. In addition, manmade laws also allowed for the stoning of the men who cheated with her. But by that time, men were off the hook and they blamed and stoned only women for adultery as they still do in various ways around the world. But YHWshua, in love, turned away her accusers and set her free saying, now go and think about what you have done, don't sin anymore, but be at peace. <u>He was gentle and loving and forgiving to this woman</u>.

Over and over throughout scripture, from cover to cover, <u>when properly translated</u>, we see YHWH's gentle love, compassion, healing and strength towards women who were hurting and in need whether physically or emotionally. It was self-righteous hypocritical people *(both men and women)* who set into place the demeaning of women as a whole. But YHWH – in His perfect 'real' love, offers hope and healing to all those who are cast down.

Psalms 34:18 - **Psalms 34:18 YHWH is nigh** *(close)* **to them that are of a broken heart; and saves such as be of a contrite** *(crushed)* **spirit.**

Cruel and selfish people in the world want to take, and in abusive situations that is even more true. They want to take a woman's freedom, her life, her dreams, her hopes, her health and her love – her very person and character, and at times, even her reason for living.

But in YHWH all things are possible and when you are in Him no one and nothing can take you out of His hands because He holds you for the precious child that you are to Him.

Not one person on the face of this earth can stop any woman from seeking the true, genuine love and healing of YHWH, the Creator – not one. People may try to stop you, they may laugh at you or try to criticize you, threaten you or try to coerce you – but YHWH has given you freewill for a purpose and He also not only heals, but strengthens.

The purpose of our freewill is to seek and find His love with a free heart, not by coercion or violence as religions and individuals have done, and still do. To have a genuine relationship with the Creator of life and that, is an amazing wonder that is open to all who desire to know and love Him.

No matter who you are, no matter your situation, you can start seeking in your heart right now – for His pure and perfect love and for healing and freedom in your life. He tells us repeatedly to never give up hope, and to lean on Him because His yoke is easy and His burden is light – unlike the world which is heavily laden with burdens to bear. All he asks is that when you seek and call on Him, that you do it with a <u>sincere heart</u> for His truth and love.

John 4:24 God *(YHWH)* **is a Spirit: and they that worship him must worship him in spirit and in truth.**

Woman – never give up hope. YHWH never designed you to be abused, He never ordained a man to *rule over* you, He never said it was okay to harm, dismiss, control, beat, berate, belittle, smash down or rape a wife! Genuine love and wisdom seeks peace in all things and genuine love does no harm.

Remember always that if you have been living in abuse and you have been told that somehow that abuse is your fault, or that all women are doomed to endure without hope of freedom because of the first woman's choices – then you have been lied to.

The accuser has indeed deceived the whole world, not only about the Name of YHWH and the Son, YHWshua, but also in many other areas including the purpose and life of women, His beautiful, intelligent and creative loving daughters.

Romans 13:10 Love works no ill *(harm, hurt)* **to his neighbor: therefore love is the fulfilling of the law.** *(The closest neighbor we have is our spouse!)*

Women are not dogs designed to follow their husband around with a collar on their neck to ensure obedience. According to the written Word of YHWH, a husband is to rise up and become the loving, caring, protector to his wife that he should have been in the beginning. He is to become a man that a woman would desire to stand at his side, love, help and follow, as a good shepherd would.

Most women will desire to honor, respect, trust and help a man who treats her with genuine love, honor, respect, dignity, faithfulness. It was never designed that a man is to pull, push, stomp, batter and belittle a woman down under his feet in order to direct her every breath and ensure that he is seen as a master over her.

Women are just as dearly loved as man in the eyes and heart of YHWH and that is according to His written Word, not my personal opinion, though I have tested His Word and believe, as I am now also a free woman in, and through, Him.

He does not call His sons and then say, 'Oh, and you can bring your wives if you want to'. NO! He calls to His daughters just as He calls to His sons!

Isaiah *(YeshaYHW)* **43:4-7** Since thou were precious in my sight, you have been honorable, and I have loved you: therefore will I give men for you, and people for your life. Fear not: for I am with you: I will bring your seed from the east, and gather you from the west; I will say to the north, Give up; and to the south, Keep not back: <u>bring my sons from far, and my daughters from the ends of the earth</u>; Even <u>every one</u> that is called by my name: for I have created him for my glory, I have formed him; yea, I have made him.

Chayil Ishah *(Strong and Valiant Women)* are precious and dearly loved in the sight of YHWH, in fact scripture says that you are a <u>gift</u> to men, <u>someone very precious, and more valuable than rubies</u>. Let no one, man or woman, ever convince you otherwise. Women are a treasure of love and wisdom with <u>many</u> gifts and talents and abilities that your Creator has given you in order to be able to help care for the Earth and each other.

Proverbs 19:14 Houses and riches are an inheritance from fathers; a wise wife is from YHWH.

Proverbs 31:10 Who can find a Chayil Ishah *(Strong and Valiant woman)* for her value is far above rubies. *(A strong and valiant woman is more valuable than rubies because she opens her mouth with wisdom and wisdom is more valuable than rubies!)*

Proverbs 31:25-26 Strength and dignity are her clothing. She delights at the time to come. <u>She opens her mouth with wisdom.</u> Faithful instruction is on her tongue.

Pslams 27 A Psalm of David *(DWD)* YHWH is my light and my salvation; whom shall I fear? YHWH is the strength of my life; of whom shall I be afraid? When the wicked, even mine enemies and my foes, came upon me to eat up my flesh *(destroy me),* they stumbled and fell. Though a host should encamp against me, my heart shall not fear: though war should rise against me, in this will I be confident. One thing have I desired of YHWH, that will I seek after; that I may dwell in the house of YHWH all the days of my life, to behold the beauty of YHWH, and to enquire in his temple. For in the time of trouble he shall hide me in his pavilion: in the secret of his tabernacle shall he hide me; he shall set me up upon a rock. And now shall mine head be lifted up above mine enemies round about me: therefore will I offer in his tabernacle sacrifices of joy; I will sing, yes, I will sing praises to YHWH. Hear, YHWH, when I cry with my voice: have mercy also upon me, and answer me. When you said, Seek you my face; my heart said to thee, Your face, YHWH, will I seek. Hide not your face far from me; put not your servant away in anger: you have been my help; leave me not, neither forsake me, O God *(Elohym)* of my salvation. When my father and my mother forsake me, then YHWH will take me up. Teach me your way, YHWH, and lead me in a plain path, because of mine enemies. Deliver me not over to the will of mine enemies: for false witnesses are risen up against me, and such as breathe out cruelty. I had fainted, unless I had believed to see the goodness of YHWH in the land of the living.

You do not need to remain in darkness anymore. YHWH is a brilliant and beautiful light of life, hope and love for all who seek Him with a sincere heart.

Have hope and take courage. Abuse is not love and YWHH, the One who created you with such love and beauty, never designed it for a man to rule 'over' you or abuse, belittle and control you.

Psalms 116 I love YHWH, because he has heard my voice and my supplications. Because he has inclined his ear to me, therefore will I call upon him as long as I live. The sorrows of death compassed me, and the pains of hell got hold upon me: I found trouble and sorrow. Then called I upon the name of YHWH; YHWH, I beseech you, deliver my soul. Gracious is YHWH, and righteous; yes, our Mighty One is merciful. YHWH preserves the simple: I was brought low, and he helped me. Return to your rest, O my soul; for YHWH has dealt bountifully with you. For you have delivered my soul from death, mine eyes from tears, and my feet from falling. I will walk before YHWH in the land of the living. I believed, therefore have I spoken: I was greatly afflicted: I said in my haste, All men are liars. What shall I render to YHWH for all his benefits toward me? I will take the cup of salvation, and call upon the name of YHWH. I will pay my vows to YHWH now in the presence of all his people. Precious in the sight of YHWH is the death of his saints. YHWH, truly I am your servant; I am your servant, and the son of your handmaid: you have loosed my bonds. I will offer to you the sacrifice of thanksgiving, and will call upon the name of YHWH. I will pay my vows unto the now in the presence of all his people, In the courts of YHWH' house, in the midst of you, O Jerusalem. Praise you YHWH.

It Is Time

It is time to sound the call,
It is time to be set free,
It is time to know the Truth,
And be who He created you to be.

It is time to walk in peace,
It is time to walk in love,
It is time to walk in strength,
And wisdom from above.

It is time to gather courage,
It is time to walk upright,
It is time to resist the lies,
It is time to stand and fight,

It is time to trust YHWH,
It is time to know His Name,
It is time to walk in freedom,
It is time to stop the blame,

It is time to seek the truth,
'Seek and you will find',
It is time to use your gifts,
It is time to renew your mind,

It is time for no more doubting,
It is time to know who you are,
It is time to know you're special,
To the One who created the stars.

It is time to be filled with wonder,
It is time, it is the hour,

To receive the light of YHWshua
And be filled with the Spirit's power.

It is time to gather confidence,
It is time to lose the doubt,
It is time to know the whole truth,
It is time to praise with a shout!

It is time to start rejoicing,
It is time to know your worth,
More precious than rubies you are,
YHWH loved you before your birth.

It is time to stop living in fear of mankind,
It is time to stop believing the lies,
It is time to rejoice in all that you are,
It's okay to laugh, or if you need, to cry.

It is time to know without any doubts,
You are Chayil Ishah,
When adopted by the Father,
The apple of His eye He saw.

People may try to stop you,
They will try to make you cower,
But gather your strength and courage in YAH,
For it is the time, it is the hour.

Copyright 2007 (Revised 2013) Cheryl Gidding

To all who have read this book – May the peace that surpasses all understanding fill you, may His love fill you to overflowing in your life and may He grant you your heart's desires as you seek Him with all your hearts. May you be FREE in Him as He designed for His sons AND daughters to be!

Blessings,

Cheryl Gidding

Notes

**…..See Chapter 2 for a detailed explanation of the Name YHWH

****…..Please note: This book is not a language or vocabulary lesson – this is truth about abuse. More Chayil Ishah books 'will' be coming which go into the nitty gritty of the language and definitions. Blessings!

1 – pg 29 - National Coalition Against Domestic Violence

2 – pg 29 - Sharmila Lawrence, National Center for Children in Poverty, Domestic Violence and Welfare Policy: *Research Findings That Can Inform Policies on Marriage and Child Well-Being* 5 (2002).

3 – pg 29 - Africana Voices Against Violence, Tufts University, Statistics, 2002

4 – pg 30 - Patricia Tjaden & Nancy Thoennes, U.S. Dep't of Just., NCJ 183781

5 – pg 30 - National Council of Child Abuse and Family Violence

6 – pg 30 - Department of Health and Human Services (HHS)

7 – pg 33 - UN Study On The Status of Women, Year 2000

8 – pg 33 – UNFPA -

9 – pg 33 - Heise

10 – pg 33 – UNFPA

11 – pg 36 - This material was reprinted/adapted from the publication titled *Religion and Domestic Violence: Information and Resources* (2007) by the National Resource Center on Domestic Violence

12 – pg 49 - The word spiral here suggests that it was from the DNA of the man's heart, or the DNA found in the 'marrow of the bone' that woman was created. The root words found in TsL'a' speak of something curved, a dark cavity, and the color of crimson red. When viewed in the proper Light one can easily see the DNA as YHWH is after all, the Creator of Life.

13 – pg 45 - The full translation of Ishah is three fold. Properly it is AShH. Most people divide the word as Ash/H. They see the first root word as Ash which means fire, they then use *'modern rules of grammar'* for the added H and they get the definition as 'woman/fire'.

However there is another meaning that has been hidden from the world and believers for centuries at minimum. The ancient pictographs did not have rules of grammar. When one divides the word AShH slightly differently one gets a VERY different meaning. Dividing it like this… A/ShH (*using the second root word found instead of the first and easiest*) it now means 'Strong equal'. Same word, same spelling, nothing is changed just looking at the 'correct' root word we see clearly that the most ancient meaning for the word Ishah (*Ashah – woman*) is 'Strong Equal'. Yes indeed – the whole world has been misled about much!

14 - pg 55 - Robert L. Wilken in the Encyclopedia Britannica

15 - .pg 56 - www.newadvent.org/fathers/

16 – pg 59 – A homonym is a word that has more than one meaning while the spelling of that word does not change. A good example is the word 'desert.'. One must use the context in order to determine the correct meaning, e.g. "The desert sand is very hot." "Do not desert your post." One means literally the hot arid climate in some regions and the other means to abruptly leave something. In the same way the Paleo-Hebrew words can have several meanings depending on the level and depth of understanding one has, or is seeking, along with context of what is being said.

Made in the USA
San Bernardino, CA
19 August 2013